Copyright © 2018 Benjamin Luster

All rights reserved. This book or any portion thereof may not be reproduced or used in any manner whatsoever without the express written permission of the publisher except for the use of brief quotations in a book review.

Printed in the United States of America

First Printing, 2018

ISBN-13: 978-1987552553

ISBN-10: 1987552555

www.pisforpoop.weebly.com

P is for Poop!

by Ben Luster

To my daughter, Annalyn.
Dad loves you.

pictures by Sarah Wash

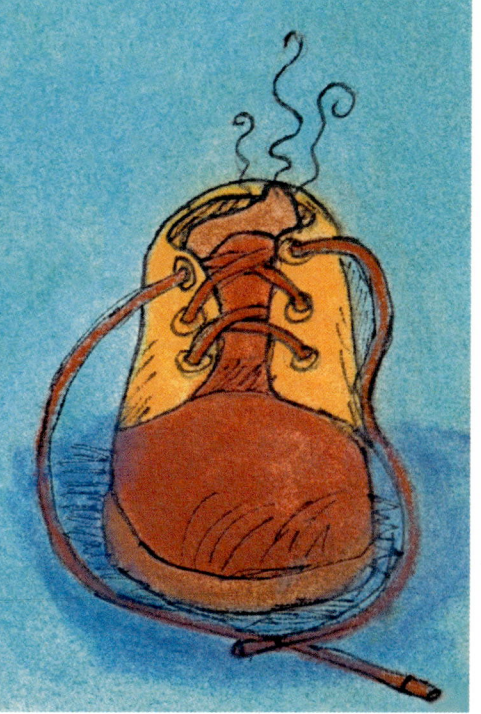

C is for Cat,
who pooped in your shoe

D is for Dog,
who pooped in there too

E is for Errands, in under an hour

G is for Gorgeous, marker art on the wall

I is for Insects that come home from school

K is for Kisses from your slobbery pet

N is for Nope; can't remember what I came in here for

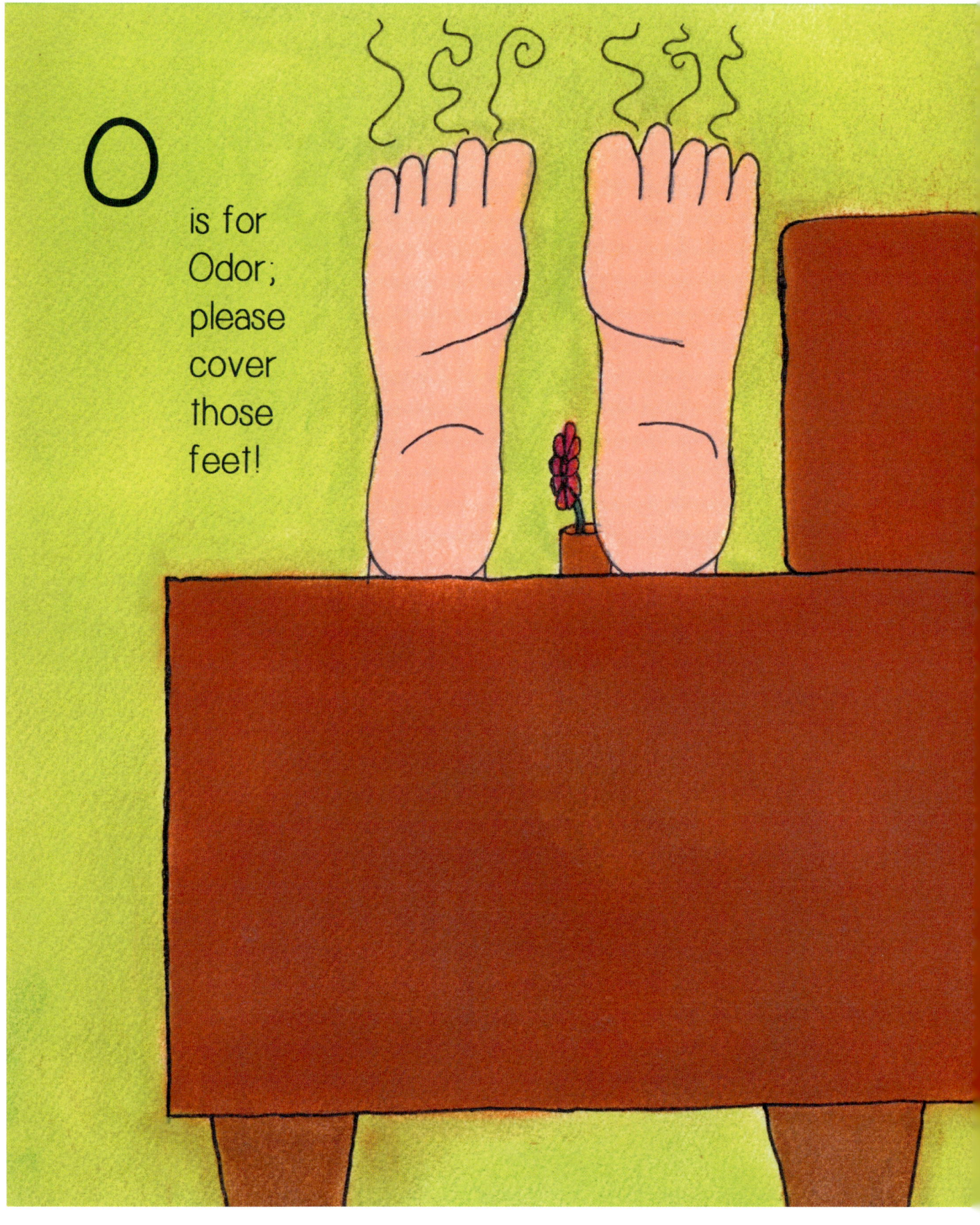

O is for Odor; please cover those feet!

Q is for Quiet, a game played in the car

R is for Ruckus;
we didn't get very far

S is for Scratching, little paws at the door

W is for Wander, in the dark we do stumble

X is for X-ray,
broken rump from the tumble

Y is for You, who makes everything right

For more children's books like
P IS FOR POOP, visit
www.pisforpoop.weebly.com

Made in the USA
Monee, IL
18 February 2020